FIGHTING FORCES IN THE AIR

F-15 EAGLE

LYNN STONE

Publishing LLC
Vero Beach, Florida 32964

www.rourkepublishing.com

PHOTO CREDITS: All photos courtesy of the U.S. Air Force

Title page: *A ground crew checks over an F-15C after a mission over Iraq in 2003.*

Editor: Frank Sloan

Library of Congress Cataloging-in-Publication Data

Stone, Lynn M.
  F-15 Eagle / Lynn M. Stone.
      p. cm. -- (Fighting forces in the air)
  Includes bibliographical references and index.
  ISBN 1-59515-181-8 (hardcover)
  1. Eagle (Jet fighter plane) I. Title. II. Series: Stone, Lynn M. Fighting forces in the air.
  UG1242.F5S783 2004
  623.74'64--dc22
                                              2004011744

Printed in the USA

CG/CG

TABLE OF CONTENTS

THE F-15 EAGLE

The twin-tailed F-15 Eagle is an extremely fast and highly **maneuverable** fighter jet designed for air superiority. Aircraft engineers designed the F-15 to be the best air-to-air combat fighter in the world.

The Eagle's superiority was developed through a combination of speed, **range**, weaponry, **avionics**, and maneuverability. It was built to out-fly and outfight any potential enemy aircraft—present or projected.

An F-15C Eagle cruises on a training flight over the Snake River in Idaho. ▶

▲
A pair of F-15E Strike Eagles join in a training mission over Idaho's Sawtooth Mountains.

Designers of the original F-15 boasted, "Not a pound for ground." That slogan meant the Eagle would be strictly an air combat machine, not a **multi-role** fighter that would also attack targets on the ground. The U.S. Air Force began to recognize, however, that the Eagle *could* be used for ground as well as air attacks if certain changes were made. Changes were made, and by 1988, the F-15E Strike Eagle had been developed and put into service.

FUNCTION: MULTI-ROLE FIGHTER; AIR-TO-AIR, AIR-TO-GROUND ATTACK AIRCRAFT

BUILDER: BOEING COMPANY

POWER SOURCE: TWO PRATT AND WHITNEY F100-PW-200 OR 229 TURBOFAN ENGINES WITH AFTERBURNERS

THRUST: 25,000-29,000 POUNDS EACH ENGINE

LENGTH: 63.8 FEET (19.4 METERS)

HEIGHT: 18.5 FEET (5.6 METERS)

WINGSPAN: 42.8 FEET (13 METERS)

SPEED: MORE THAN 1,875 MILES PER HOUR (3,000 KILOMETERS)

CEILING: 65,000 FEET (19,812 METERS)

MAXIMUM TAKEOFF WEIGHT: 81,000 POUNDS (36,486 KILOGRAMS)

RANGE: MORE THAN 3,500 MILES (5,600 KILOMETERS)

CREW: TWO

DATE DEPLOYED: APRIL, 1988

The Strike Eagle's **airframe** is similar to the F-15 Eagle's, but in many ways it is an altogether different aircraft. Unlike the F-15, the Strike Eagle carries two crew members, a pilot and a weapon systems officer (WSO). And unlike the F-15, the Strike Eagle is a multi-role aircraft.

The primary mission of the Strike Eagle is to drop weapons accurately on targets. The Strike Eagle is built to fight its way to a long distance site, destroy its target, and, if necessary, fight its way home.

The F-15E requires a crew of two—the pilot and a weapons system officer.

The original F-15s were designated F-15As by the U.S. Air Force. A second version of the F-15, the F-15B, was a two-seat Eagle. The second seat was for an instructor pilot, not for a WSO. F-15Bs are often flown with empty rear cockpits.

The F-15C is an improved version of the F-15A. It has greater internal fuel capacity, new avionics, and advanced weapons. The F-15D is an improved version of the original two-seat F-15B.

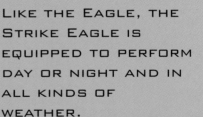

FACT FILE ★

LIKE THE EAGLE, THE STRIKE EAGLE IS EQUIPPED TO PERFORM DAY OR NIGHT AND IN ALL KINDS OF WEATHER.

▲

An F-15C Eagle fires an AIM-7 Sparrow, a medium-range, air-to-air missile.

Like other American warplanes, F-15s continually undergo modifications to bring their safety features, avionics, and weaponry up to date.

CHAPTER TWO

F-15s gain their maneuverability through a design that provides a combination of powerful thrust from the airplane's twin engines coupled with a low wing loading **ratio**. Wing loading is the ratio of weight to wing size. Consider another air-to-air fighter, the falcon. The falcon is a hawk that hunts other birds in flight. A falcon has broad wings but a relatively light body. A swan's wings are much larger than a falcon's, but its weight in proportion to its wing size is much greater. The falcon has a lower wing loading ratio, so it is a much more **agile** flyer than a swan.

An F-15 Eagle roars over Nellis Air Force Base, Nevada. ▶

The F-15, of course, does not maneuver itself. That is the pilot's responsibility. And the pilot is aided by advanced avionics that include a heads-up display system (HUD) visible in any light. With a HUD, a pilot never has to look down.

▲
Broad wings and powerful twin engines give F-15s extra maneuverability and speed.

Surrounded by high-tech flight systems, an F-15 pilot watches his ground chief as the plane readies for takeoff.

F-15s are also equipped with advanced systems in radar, communications, instrument landing, and electronic **countermeasures** to combat enemy missiles. In addition, they have a system to identify other aircraft as "friend or foe."

RADAR CAN ALSO PICK OUT A LOW-FLYING AIRCRAFT 30,000 FEET (9,144 METERS) BELOW THE STRIKE EAGLE.

In the highly advanced F-15E, pilots have the APG-70 radar system. It can provide information about range, altitude, and airspeed of other aircraft more than 100 miles (162 km) away. The APG-70 also allows pilots to detect ground targets at longer ranges. On a display screen, the system will identify bridges or airfields more than 80 miles (130 km) distant.

For the Strike Eagle's weapons officer, the rear cockpit has four display screens. They provide radar, electronic warfare information, and a "moving" map for navigation. They also have information about targets, the Strike Eagle's weapons, and other aircraft. Like the pilot, the weapons officer enjoys an eye-level HUD.

◄ *Behind the green-tinted HUD (Heads-Up Display), the pilot brings his F-15C up to the boom of a KC-135 air tanker for mid-air refueling.*

For night operations, a cockpit screen displays a surprisingly good view of objects in the night. This is made possible by an FLIR **infrared** sensor system.

WSOs have at their controls a radar warning receiver, radar jammer, and an automatic chaff dispenser. Jammers send signals to confuse enemy radar. And chaff—bits of metal released into the air—creates a false image on enemy radar screens.

▲
High-tech systems aboard this F-15 help a pilot know precisely when to release the AIM-7 Sparrow missile.

High altitude flight helps F-15s and other aircraft conserve fuel.

A pilot can fly an F-15 at more than two and one-half times the speed of sound (**Mach** 2.5), or approximately 1,875 miles (3,037 km) per hour. But extremely high-speed flight is rarely necessary, or desirable. Eagles and Strike Eagles are generally flown at **subsonic** speeds. Aircraft burn extreme amounts of fuel at high speeds, and that reduces their range. With extra fuel tanks, F-15s have a range of about 3,450 miles (5,590 km). Strike Eagles, in ideal conditions, can exceed 3,500 miles (5,670 km) between refueling operations.

FIREPOWER

The F-15 can carry a variety of air-to-air weaponry. The pilot operates weapons controls from the engine throttles and the control stick. HUD visuals help the pilot change from one weapons system to another.

The Eagle can be armed with various missile combinations that attach to the plane's frame. It may have four AIM-9L/M Sidewinder and four AIM-7F/M Sparrow missiles or eight AIM-120 AMRAAMs (advanced medium range air-to-air missiles).

FACT FILE ★

THE EAGLE HAS A 20MM WING-MOUNTED GATLING GUN.

An F-15C undergoes mid-air refueling from an air tanker. ▶

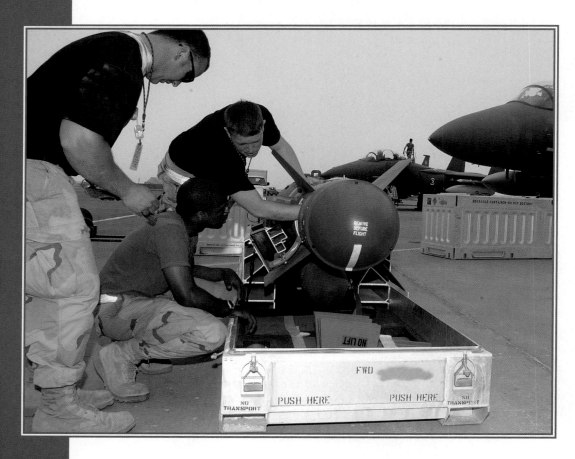

▲ Bomb loaders prepare to mount an air-to-ground missile (AGM-130) to a Strike Eagle wing.

The Strike Eagle can carry a similar network of air-to-air missiles, but it also can carry almost any air-to-ground weapon the Air Force has. Among them are **munitions** that are guided by lasers, electronic systems, or infrared. One such weapon is the 300-pound (136-kg) Maverick air-to-ground missile. Another powerful F-15E weapon is the laser-guided GBU-28 bomb, a 5,000-pound (2,268-kg) monster nicknamed the "**Bunker** Buster." F-15Es can also deliver the Joint Direct Attack Munition (JDAM), a "smart" bomb guided by satellite signals.

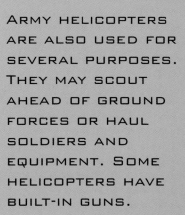

FACT FILE ★

ARMY HELICOPTERS ARE ALSO USED FOR SEVERAL PURPOSES. THEY MAY SCOUT AHEAD OF GROUND FORCES OR HAUL SOLDIERS AND EQUIPMENT. SOME HELICOPTERS HAVE BUILT-IN GUNS.

One of the Strike Eagle's most important systems for weapons delivery is LANTIRN. LANTIRN is the acronym for Lockheed Martin Company's Low Altitude Navigation and Targeting Infrared for Night system. This system allows pilots safe low altitude flight by using information that LANTIRN directs to the HUD screen. Radar and laser technology in the system identify ground terrain and also mark enemy targets up to 10 miles (16 km) away. LANTIRN allows an F-15E to make remarkably accurate strikes on enemy targets.

▲
An F-15E Strike Eagle releases a 5,000-pound (2,268-kg) laser-guided "Bunker Buster."

▲
A U.S. Air Force mechanic inspects the engines and twin exhausts of an F-15.

The F-15 is powered by two turbofan engines with afterburners for acceleration. Each of these engines develops about 23,450 pounds of thrust. The F15-E has a pair of Pratt and Whitney F100-PW-229 turbofan engines, each producing about 29,000 pounds of thrust.

CHAPTER FOUR

In the late 1960s, during the war in Vietnam, the U.S. Air Force began plans for a new, high-performance fighter jet. American Phantom II fighters flying in Vietnam at that time were used largely for air-to-ground missions. They had some difficulty combating the much smaller and more maneuverable Soviet-built MiG fighters flown by the North Vietnamese.

▲

Air National Guard F-15As fly in a weapons system evaluation program.

The McDonnell Douglas Company, later joined with the Boeing Company, was chosen to build the new air superiority fighter. The first F-15 was delivered to the Air Force in January, 1976. The first F-15C and D models were delivered in 1979.

Eagles and Strike Eagles were used during the Gulf War (Operation Desert Storm) in 1991. F-15Cs accounted for 34 of the Air Force's 37 air victories. F-15E Strike Eagles, equipped with LANTIRN, were used primarily at night to hunt missile launchers and artillery sites.

▲

F-15E drops Mark 84 laser-guided bombs over a Nevada testing range.

▲

An F-15E Strike Eagle pilot's green HUD shows through the clear canopy.

F-15s were later used to patrol the United Nations' no-fly zone in southern Iraq and in support of NATO (North Atlantic Treaty Organization) operations in Bosnia. More recently, 48 Strike Eagles and 42 Eagles were among the USAF fighters used during Operation Iraqi Freedom in March and April, 2003.

FLYING INTO THE FUTURE

Even high-tech fighters like the F-15 become **obsolete**. They will gradually be replaced by even better fighters, including the F-22 Raptor, which began service in 2004. Boeing expected its last and most advanced F-15Es to be manufactured in 2004.

Nevertheless, the U.S. Air Force expects to have approximately 130 combat-ready F-15s until about 2016. But by 2030, if not before, plans are to have the entire F-15 inventory replaced by new jets.

▲
The F/A-22 Raptor will eventually replace the Air Force's Eagles and Strike Eagles.

Glossary

agile (AJ ul) — highly maneuverable; able to complete quick, graceful movements

airframe (AIR FRAYM) — the wings and shell, or body, of an airplane without its engines or weapons

avionics (AY vee ON iks) — the electronic systems and devices used in aviation

bunker (BUN kur) — a strengthened, underground chamber for soldiers

countermeasures (KAUNT ur MEZH urz) — any number of strategies and systems used to avoid being struck by enemy fire

infrared (IN fruh RED) — (also known as *thermal radiation* or *infrared rays*) the invisible-to-the-naked-eye energy rays given off by any warm object, such as a human being, battle tank, or airplane; invisible heat rays that can be detected by special instruments

Mach (MAWK) — a high speed expressed by a Mach number; Mach 1 is the speed of sound

maneuverable (muh NYUV ur uh bul) — able to make changes in direction and position for a specific purpose

multi-role (MULL tee ROLL) — capable of being used in more than one way

munitions (MYU nish unz) — ammunition

obsolete (OB so LEET) — no longer current; out-of-date

range (RAYNJ) — the distance an aircraft can fly without refueling

ratio (RAY shee OH) — a mathematical relationship between two or more things

subsonic (SUB son ik) — any speed below the speed of sound

INDEX

FURTHER READING

Green, Gladys and Michael. *Tactical Fighters: The F-15 Eagles.* Capstone, 2003

Holden, Henry. *Air Force Aircraft*. Enslow, 2001

WEBSITES TO VISIT

http://www.fas.org/man/dod-101/sys/ac/f-15.htm

http://www.af.mil/factsheets

ABOUT THE AUTHOR

Lynn M. Stone is the author of more than 400 children's books. He is a talented natural history photographer as well. Lynn, a former teacher, travels worldwide to photograph wildlife in its natural habitat.